MY CHOSEN PATH

PAINTING IN THE LANDSCAPE

I traipse over frosted fields, anticipation burning in my chest,
In search of my spot, laden with easel, stool and the rest!
As dawn breaks the sun's rosy fingers caress the frosted forms,
I am at work, fighting the cold and canvas; the artist performs.

Into the fray I am thrust, headlong into a battle, in my ability I trust,
Against the time and light, "more yellow here" and so I adjust.
The sky is done, the trees I've begun, now comes the fun,
Skeletal forms against the sky, needs a slight touch, not to ruin my run.

The sun hangs higher in the sky, shadows retreat, my patience is tried,
With painting almost complete, barely feeling my feet, who said this job was easy has lied.
Though the rules are clear, to paint sky like the sky and a tree like a tree,
Constable quotes 'landscape painting at its best is a branch of philosophy'.

I wander back home, over melted fields with contentment in my heart,
To paint plein air, is as simple and as difficult as that... that is art!
My painting is finished, all canvas covered, landscape finally captured,
The painting is placed upon my easel and scrutinised, 'that light mastered'.

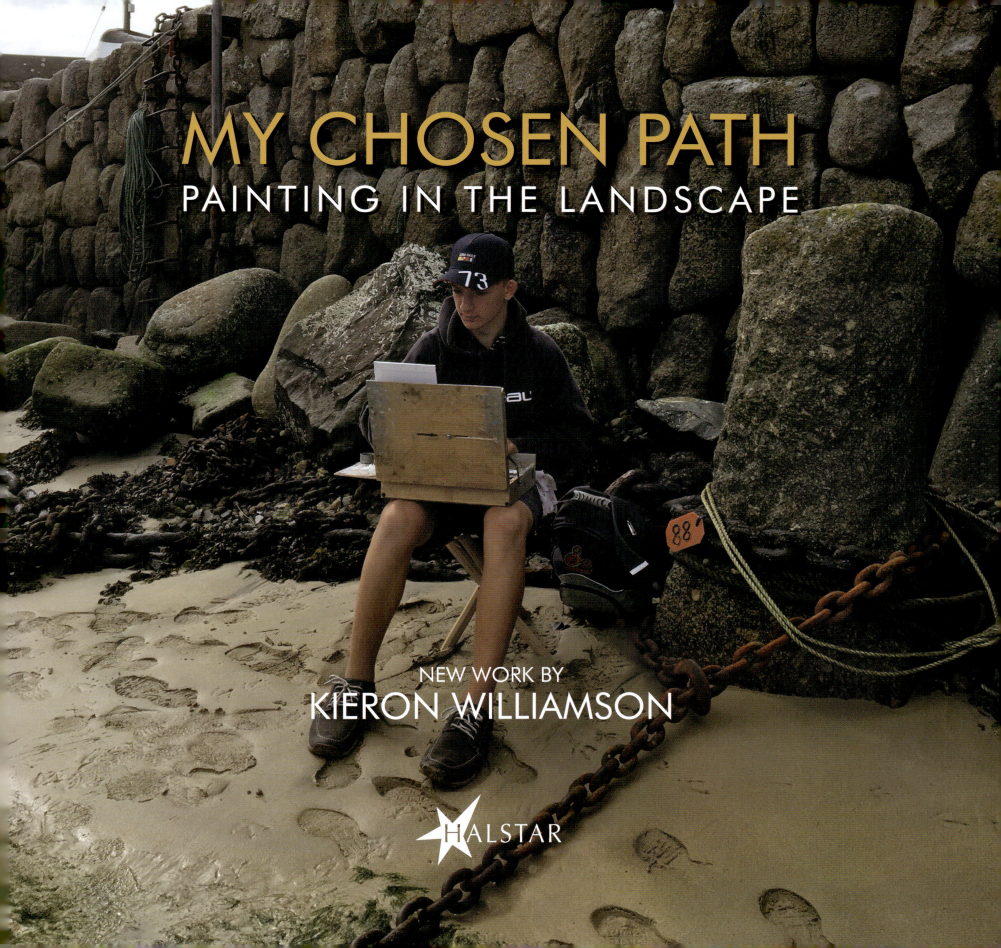

MY CHOSEN PATH

PAINTING IN THE LANDSCAPE

NEW WORK BY
KIERON WILLIAMSON

HALSTAR

First published in Great Britain in 2018
Copyright © 2018 Kieron Williamson
Final chapter text copyright © 2018 Simon Butler

British Library Cataloguing-in-Publication Data
A CIP record for this title is available from the British Library

ISBN 978 1 906690 66 3

HALSTAR
Halsgrove House, Ryelands Business Park,
Bagley Road, Wellington, Somerset TA21 9PZ
Tel: 01823 653777   Fax: 01823 216796
email: sales@halsgrove.com

An imprint of Halstar Ltd, part of the halsgrove group
of companies. Information on all Halsgrove titles is
available at: www.halsgrove.com

Printed in India by Parksons Graphics Ltd

FOREWORD
By Ken Howard OBE, RA

I DON'T THINK there is a bushel which could hide Kieron Williamson's talent. The skills he has so readily acquired, he means to use. This exercise is as necessary to him as drink is to the drunkard. Kieron is a true painter.

In the arts it is necessary to start early and Kieron has certainly fulfilled that requirement. Art must always be life enhancing, we are here for a relatively short time and anything that makes time richer is worthwhile. Kieron's work certainly enriches our lives.

Painting is about revelation and Kieron shows us the world in his terms; it is also about celebration and Kieron celebrates the world. Finally it is about communication and Kieron speaks to us unequivocally.

Kieron lives in a difficult period. He has no time for the distain, even contempt, for the gifts of drawing and objective painting conveyed by critics who drag their weary eyes round exhibition after exhibition for twenty years or so before sinking into oblivion. His vision will continue to delight the eye of the lover of the visual arts.

This is a good moment to look back over Kieron Williamson's work, not only for the pleasure such work gives but also for the encouragement it extends to those who, sometimes overawed by the pretentions of those dominating the world in Art, may feel released and able to say, this I like, this pleases, this does me good.

And it leaves us with a lovely question – what lies ahead?

Ken Howard
Mousehole 2018

ACKNOWLEDGEMENTS

MY FAMILY AND I WOULD LIKE TO express heartfelt thanks to all those who have offered their support. To family members who have kept us grounded. To our good friends Neil and Jane for their limitless enthusiasm, wisdom and guidance. To Carol Ann Pennington for being a constant source of support and spiritual guidance. To Brian Ryder ROI PIEA, for those early enjoyable art classes and to Tony and Gaynor Garner for their friendship and good humour. To David Curtis ROI, RSMA, Trevor Chamberlain ROI, RSMA, Bert Wright PPRSMA, FRSA and Prof. Ken Howard OBE, RA for their time and constructive critiques during several painting days in Cornwall and Norfolk. To Kimberley Walker IEA for being a great source of inspiration and for the fun ideas shared with Billie-Jo. To Jan Sorrell our accountant, who deserves tea and medals every quarter! To Natalie Gray, ITV, for being a great friend and our unrivalled link to local media. To Tony Aldous, ITV, Wally and Sheri Webb, BBC Radio for taking us messing about in boats on The Broads. To Caroline and Ray at the *Holt Chronicle*. To Matt Doughty and Steve Stokes, Boudicca Marketing for the website and technical support throughout the years. To Dawn Gerber, BBC, for her support and time shared with us. To Alban Donohoe and Jeremy Heaton for their professional photography and technical support, it is appreciated! Sincere thanks go to Michael and Teresa Hill and all the staff at Picturecraft framing and the art shop for their constant support and recommendations and for the time and encouragement they offer young Billie-Jo. Special thanks go to Adrian and Clare Hill for their tireless support and enthusiastic representation of my work and Billie-Jo's jewellery at The Gallery, Picturecraft, Holt. Thanks to Val, Jade and Natalie for their care and sensitivity at our most stressful times, and to Bernard for his mystery photos that keep me musing over the wonders of the world. Thanks to Beryl Knowles (our very own fountain of knowledge) for her flexibility and enthusiasm and for making home education a complete joy for us all. To our dear neighbours Tom and Doreen for being there when we need them. Sincere thanks to Simon and Anna Butler for their friendship and for Simon's unrivalled stories and support! To Nicky and Gavin Dollard, Delamore Arts, Devon, for their hospitality over the years and their unequalled support for the arts. Thanks must go to Will Amley, Bob Clabon, Will and John Puncher and Michael Flood – local farmers who allow me access to their barns, cattle and horses; also to NE&PC livery yard, Swafield, for allowing Kieron to paint their horses regularly and take photos. Thanks to Penlee House Gallery and Museum, Penzance. The Munnings Art Museum, Dedham. Thanks to Bill, Barbara and Faye Hawkins, Port Isaac Pottery for their time and support. Thanks Barbara for coming painting with me, we must do it again! Big thanks to Cheryl, Port Isaac for being our angel! To Chris and the team at Chapel Café for great food and great coffee! Thanks to Sylvia Johns-Pender and Tim Pender for taking me out on *Ellen* (an 1882 17-foot Gorran Haven Crabber owned by the Cornish Maritime Trust), and to artists Tim Hall and Henrietta Graham, Mousehole, for their time and encouragement. To the Tyler Gallery, Mousehole, for keeping me inspired! Thanks always must go to the thousands of supporters and private collectors across the globe that make all this possible and who have sent so many kind words of support, appreciation and guidance, and for sharing with us their own stories of being inspired to return to their brushes. Scarcely a day goes by when I don't paint, think about painting, or scan the landscape around me searching for the next painting. All this remains possible because of the support and encouragement that my parents and my younger sister still offer me unconditionally.

Kieron Williamson
Trunch, Norfolk 2018

INTRODUCTION
By Kieron Williamson

PAINTING FOR ME is all about portraying the way that the light falls upon the landscape. To recreate it in my own style by painting outside, en plein air, is my constant challenge. I have been trying to do this ever since that first evening when I sat on the beach wall at Gillan in Cornwall with my drawing pad and pencils and tried to recreate what captured my heart. I was just five years old.

I am lucky enough to be surrounded by landscapes and scenery that give me such a burning desire to paint them. From the charming historical market town of Holt with its beautiful High Street and church, to the marshes full of cattle, the Norfolk Broads scattered with sails at Ludham and to the patchwork of fields and barnyards. From farmers and horses that surround me in North Norfolk, there is a never ending supply of subjects and each of these landscapes change with the coming seasons.

The subject matter and my way of working I think has changed considerably. When I was about eight, Edward Seago was a huge inspiration and my paintings reflected that: big skies over the marshes, painted quickly and directly. Rarely would I revisit pieces of work, once the moment left me, that was it, and my work would either be discarded, archived or sold if I felt it was good enough. My palette is as close to the natural colours I see as I can get it; colour is important to me, more so than the composition or the subject matter at times. It was Seago's palette that drew me as much to his paintings as the subject matter, and I never tire of looking at his work.

But now I can spend up to a month working from sketches to complete larger studio paintings. I'm now taking inspiration from artists such as A. J. Munnings, George Clausen and some of the Newlyn School artists. I look for subjects similar to theirs, horses, old farmers and fishermen. The noticeable transition in my work from painting landscapes to painting people, I think was an unconscious transition, arising from being surrounded by characterful farmers, horse owners and fishermen, just as the many deceased artists painted all those years ago. I find people are so generous in allowing me to paint and photograph them, and I get so inspired by their everyday lives, such as our neighbours planting potatoes and hoeing weeds, or people working on their allotments. These are subjects I could paint all day.

MIST, FOWEY
16x16", oil canvas

Opposite:
CARRIAGE RIDE THROUGH BLICKLING
16x22", oil on canvas

I like the composition in this. The difficulty was painting the wheels, but several sketches helped me with this. I added a slight frost on the ground to show how absolutely freezing it was!

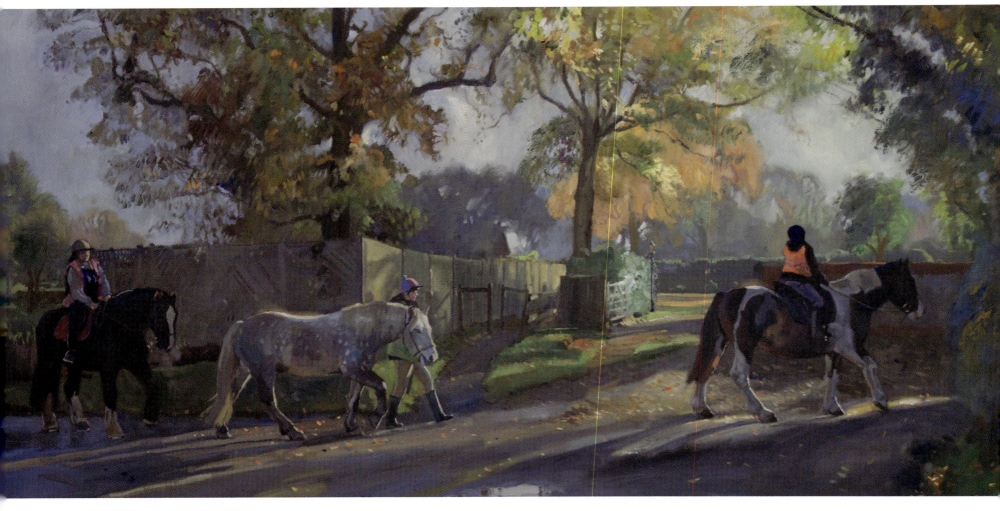

WRIGHTS LOKE WALK
20x40", oil on canvas

As soon as I saw this subject I knew I was going to paint it. This is almost the view I get from my studio window. Often on the weekends horses trot past and I rush out to get photos, but most of the time they're too far down the road! The long thin format worked perfectly for this. The painting is all about the effects of the light you get on bright autumnal mornings.

Starting large studio paintings is always an anxious time. I sit and think about it until I almost talk myself out of painting it. But I revisit the sketches I made and study the photographs I took, sometimes returning to the location to reacquaint myself with it again; getting the smells, sounds and the atmosphere back in my system. I then start drawing it out with a big mug of coffee beside me and music playing. For my larger studio works, I use linen canvas on a stretcher, the tooth of the grain being perfect for my style. I prepare the canvas with two coats of gesso. Once that has dried I put on a turpsy wash of French ultramarine, burnt sienna and a touch of titanium white. I leave that to dry for up to a week, leaving a nice dry surface to work on. After drawing it out, I stand back looking carefully for data points to work from, to make sure the heights of things are correct. Then it's into the fun bit – the paint is very thin and loose and I begin by blocking in the painting, this is the first base. I let that dry, always correcting my drawing, then slowly build the colours up. I work on no particular places first, only saving my favourite bits until last. I let the painting dry and stand and I live with it for a while before I make any changes to it, knowing that if I completely mess it up, I can wipe the paint off and the paint layer underneath is safe! I sometimes struggle knowing when to stop, that's the really hard bit.

It's important also to come back to the painting with fresh eyes, to take a break from it and do something completely different. I play football or go out on my bike. But whenever I return to the painting I see it with fresh eyes and a renewed interest and it helps to improve my work.

FLOWING THOUGHTS
18x24", oil on canvas

The deep ultramarine blue water against the bright, intense green grass challenged me, but I revelled in the challenge. I love painting the movement upon the water, the way it foams and convulses while zig-zagging currents reflect the bright blue sky.

CROSSING THE BRIDGE
20x30", oil on board

I got the idea for this painting whilst standing on a sluice gate type of mechanism. I was mid flow in my painting, everything was going well, when a tentative young cow walked across the bridge in front of me. I added the three cows on the left from sketches I made. Everything in this scene is perfect, I couldn't have imagined it any better!

'89

Study for Crossing the Bridge KCW17

KCW17

- Cattle -

I can still remember my first completed plein air painting – it was a dyke at Salthouse Marsh. It is one of a small collection of my paintings that hang in our house. It is very rare for me to complete a painting that I'm actually pleased with! Although painted about seven or eight years ago it has a lovely atmosphere, and Seago clearly was an inspiration.

The most memorable outings are the freezing cold frosty mornings, although physically challenging they often produce the best results once finished, my favourites being 'Late for Lunch', 'It Was Quiet' and 'Sunlit Copse'.

I generally wake up about 7am in the winter to paint the sunrise, only usually a walk or short bike ride away, although cycling is a bit dodgy with the roads covered in ice! I've learned over time that it is so important to dress sensibly – shooting gloves, a good thick jacket, a woolly hat or trapper hat, long socks and walking boots are the essentials, with sometimes two pairs of trousers and socks. And probably more importantly, a flask filled with hot chocolate!

Paintings are like windows, and I could never be without them.

STUDIES OF JOHN PUNCHER
7x3.75, pastel

The brightness of pigment in pastels make them nice to work with. They were perfect for catching the reflected light from the barn on John's face.

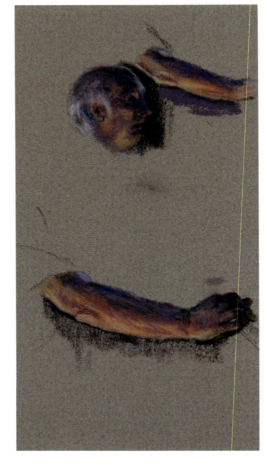

THROUGH THE MIST
12x12", oil on board

I'm glad my ability to paint horses has improved! But the aim was to capture the impressions of movement and light.

HARD GRAFT
20x24", oil on canvas

This was painted almost to remind me of what a great day this was. I biked to the farm hoping I'd see the Puncher Brothers loading up the bales. I was in luck. I spent the morning photographing and helping them load up the bales. I need to work on my pitchfork skills though!

Study For
Hard Graft

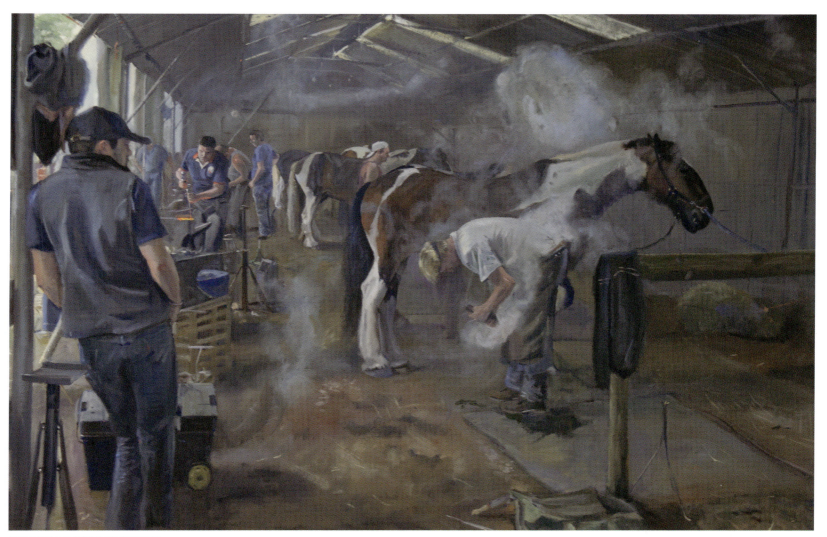

SHOEING THE HORSES
24x36", oil on canvas

This is one of the best subjects and compositions I have ever been able to paint. I found this subject whilst wandering round the Royal Norfolk Showground. Dad and I were about to leave when smoke filled the room and thus this amazing atmosphere appeared. This was one of the most complicated paintings I've ever done, but the challenge and effort have been rewarded with a painting I'm very proud of.

But in the summer, especially in Cornwall, Dad and I are up at quarter to five in the mornings to paint the sunrise and more often than not we're out in the evenings until well after nine painting the sunset. Definitely mornings and evenings give the best light. Summer is for enjoying, for swimming and for holidays. The greens are too strong and full at the height of summer and can kill a piece of work. However, if the subject matter is there, then it's worth the discomfort of the greens!

I could make it easier for myself and paint twee, chocolate-box paintings, scenes depicting a warm sunny day, where all the colours are jarring and vivid. But my paintings would not be as good or give me as much pleasure. There would be no subtlety or atmosphere and I'd be painting the same things as many other artists before me. So painting at sunrise or in the evening where there is a softer palette of colours, pinks, oranges and greys – it's these colours that I love to paint with. There is a much wider range of tones within them depending on the light effects and the weather, and I love to find hidden subjects, things that people haven't painted too often before.

Painting for me is all about portraying the way that the light falls upon the landscape

MOONLIT ISLAND
8x8", oil on board

At 10 o'clock at night the last thing Dad would want to do is go out painting! But he did and I painted this at the Rock Pool Café, Mousehole, at the top of the steps that lead down to the beach , using a floodlight to paint under. I was chuffed with the outcome and pleased I had done a good painting at such a time of night. The story attached to this piece will make it a memorable one.

Cornwall is a very special place for me, as it was here that I first started to draw. I love the light in Cornwall, it's very silvery and intense. The landscapes are the complete opposite to Norfolk, hills replace the skies, the sea depicts a whole range of blue hues and every couple of miles there is another cove or fishing port to explore. Tin mines replace trees on the north coast, and shining slate roofs contrast with Norfolk's red brick and pantiles.

Mousehole is one of my favourite places to paint. The iconic view is through the harbour entrance, but going there so much, I've found little street scenes and different views of the harbour. There are always boats out in Mount's Bay and it's nice to watch the weather fronts coming in over the Lizard, and even when it's raining in Mousehole there is always sun breaking through, lighting up the sea. We always carry a camera wherever we go, the light can change in an instant and to be there to witness it is what makes it all worthwhile.

Staying for so long in a few chosen places in Cornwall allows us to get to know various characters, like Tim Pender a local resident of Mousehole. We were invited out on a boat with Tim, an 1832 Gorran Haven crabber, called *Ellen*. It was our last evening in Mousehole and just by chance Dad passed Tim having a pint outside the Legion where they arranged for Mum and me to go out on the boat. It was a beautiful evening as we left the sanctuary of the harbour, but Tim's hat soon blew off and was never retrieved… the mizzen snapped and the mainsail got snagged and far too frequently we were very close to taking on seawater. Then the skies blackened, the wind gained in strength and rain started to fall! Thankfully, though we felt safe being with such an accomplished sailor, with Tim deciding not to push his luck anymore, we returned. But as we approached the harbour mouth, the

UNLOADING THE CATCH
20x16", oil on board

CLIFF STUDY BOSCASTLE
5x7", oil on board

Painted while perched on a cliff ledge above Boscastle harbour in 30°C heat in full sun. I like the almost silhouetted form of the cliff against the sky. I was influenced by Singer Sargent and this painting was an experimental piece.

wind was blowing straight through the gap and Tim couldn't skull against the force. We anchored up and waited for the winds to decrease, when some Mousehole fishermen offered to tow us back into the harbour in return for a pint. Tim was mortified, he'd never been towed in before! Despite the bad weather I had an amazing time and I would do it again. I took plenty of photos and I've got masses of material to work from.

When travelling back home, passing through so many counties I see so much I want to paint: old barns, cattle and rivers. But travelling home one day we saw a large encampment of gypsies (Roma). Dad stopped and Mum and I went to ask if we might take some photos. They had all the horses beside the wagons with lovely scenery behind. I love the proper Romany gypsies and their philosophy of life and freedom. As soon as I got home I started a large watercolour of the wagons and horses. Sir A. J. Munnings was a looming influence! I was thankful that the satnav had taken us that way! On a more recent occasion, I couldn't believe my luck when driving from Boscastle to Port Isaac we passed another encampment beside the road. Dad again stopped and mum and I walked and asked them if it was okay to get some photos. The intense light, wagon, horses and the overall composition were perfect. There was a really characterful man chopping kindling, a few lurcher dogs and a dark haired girl sitting in the shade in the long grass with her dogs beside a horse. When we arrived back in Norfolk I completed a large oil of them.

I have met up several times with contemporary artists David Curtis, Trevor Chamberlain, Bert Wright and Andy Hucclesbee in Cornwall for a day's painting. It is always a day filled with good humour and inspiration, being surrounded by such great artists in such beautiful surroundings. Painting can be lonely sometimes, so it's nice to meet up with like-minded artists who see the world as I do. I also paint with Port Isaac's artist Barbara Hawkins, often together on the north coast but in Penpol and Mousehole too. There was a particularly memorable day in Boscastle. It was so hot when we completed our first painting perched on the valley edge, we retreated to the shade, had an ice cream and completed our second painting with our bare feet dipped in the Valency stream that runs down into the harbour.

With Norfolk being my home county there is undoubtedly a bond with the landscape I have grown up with. The skies are unbeatable and my paintings are all influenced by the sky. When I was younger I painted extensively at Morston Quay. Dad would drive me there in the winter to catch the sunrise over Blakeney church. The puddles would been frozen over and the marshland birds would be shrilling. I have many happy memories painting there.

We moved to Ludham in 2011, a beautiful village on the Norfolk Broads. My work changed from creeks to rivers. St Benet's Abbey is still my favourite painting location. There is an eerie atmosphere that surrounds the mill and cattle graze on the fields among the undulating remains of the flint walls that formed part of the monastery that once stood here.

The tale of the Ludham dragon was the inspiration for the Break charity, GoGoDragon. I painted the scenery of Ludham, including St Benet's Abbey – and the late Eric Edwards who was a reed cutter at How Hill, and kindly invited me to observe him reed cutting. I got a great many photos and did some oil sketches. He was a lovely person and great character.

SIR JOHN ALFRED ARNESBY BROWN (1866-1955) RA. 'THE BLACK MILL' 17.5x21.5", oil on canvas

This was the first Arnesby Brown picture we bought. I really like the sky in this painting.

Opposite:
UNDER THE CORNISH SUN
40x30", oil on canvas

I painted this beautiful scene from photos I took of these gypsies, seen on the side of a road in Cornwall. I was so inspired by the light and composition, I had to paint it straight away. I didn't want to copy a Munnings, or a Laura Knight, or a Roland Wheelwright, I painted this because I saw it and was inspired to put it down on canvas. This painting is quite different to others I've done in the past.

SHADOWS RETREAT
10x14" oil on board

The Last Day on Autumn Pastures

Grazing gently on luscious grass with its dew-sweetened taste,
timelessly they nose their wet snouts over the ground.
Contrary their painful-whipping tails lash at flies with such haste,
one by one they gather on St Benet's ancient mound,
where the autumn sun seeps into their backs brightly,
and from the mound with it's hidden brick and flint a cross penetrates the sky.
To the top they now walk the whole herd forthrightly,
sky alive with starling in murmuration, scenes of geese chattering as they fly.

'Tis noon, it cometh more gentle than a spring sapling with growing leaf bud,
its warmth much stronger than its presence in the sky above.
The gentle giants sit in springy reeds and slowly chew the sodden cud,
young calfs nestled amongst mothers, as tightly as warm glove.
They stare longingly towards distant fields as green as pastures new,
farm and Ludham church on horizon, hidden by mist low-lying.
Ploughed fields damp in furrow, with near-naked copse shielding the view,
frozen dew spreads across the marsh as cattle nestle down snorting, sighing.

The setting sun reluctantly retracts her talons of warm milky rays,
stage settings altered now to dark night, no longer day.
Moon in full above sleeping herd casts a bright silver shadow maze,
glitter scattered on delicate reed heads even on mighty bull, Charolais.
His mammoth presence imposing on this cold moonlit night,
and the morning will force return of herd to manger until New Year.
Rest my grand and graceful beasts, so peaceful tis this sight;
alas new day brings no cattle but winter chill and unwelcome tear.

Written by Kieron Williamson 2015, aged twelve years.

UNLOADING THE BALES
14x10", oil on board

HEIGHT OF SUMMER
18x24", oil on canvas

I love the stances of all three horses, and the detail of the farrier. Mr Flood stands patiently whilst Rupert has his hooves attended to.

Part of the reason we moved to Ludham was that it was the home of Edward Seago. It was a huge inspiration to paint in the same places as he did, and walk past his house as we went painting, several times painting his house from the road. Whenever I am at Ludham I feel like I am walking into one of his paintings, especially on the Ludham Marshes. As I walk around them and see small dykes edged by reeds, beside an old tree and cattle grazing in the distance, I am reminded of many Seago paintings.

We moved to our current village, after living only a year at Ludham, outgrowing the house quite considerably. It's a beautiful place surrounded by farmland, livestock and is a ten minute bike ride away from the beach. There are endless painting possibilities with different light effects at different times of the year, and plenty of backroads to cycle down. It was during a cycle ride one summer's day I met Mike Flood, a wonderful character and owner of three Shire horses. I saw him standing beside his horses while they were having their hooves trimmed. I hopped over the fence and Mike told me all about his horses and kindly agreed to me taking plenty of photos. I'm always nervous asking people if I can get a photo of them as I can never guess their reactions, but from that chance meeting with Mr Flood I need not have worried. I spent a month painting 'The Height of Summer' and 'The Ploughman's Knot'.

By happenstance again on a cycle ride with Dad on a cold January day a few years ago, I first encountered the farming brothers Will and John Puncher. We came across a barn on the right-hand side of the road, a tin barn on the left, and a bit further down a thatched converted

FARM FRESH POTATOES
20x24", oil on canvas

For this piece I used two sketches, one done, in oil, on location, and a larger watercolour. These helped me produce this expressive painting. I used a photograph to ensure everything was correct. I love the strong March light casting strong, plum shadows.

My landscapes are all painted either plein air or from sketches or photographs that I've taken.

barn in the distance, where I stopped to take a photo. We could hear what sounded like a car engine, but it wasn't a car. We cycled a few more yards and I saw an old farmer, wearing a cap and a dirty high-vis jacket. Then further on behind the farmer I noticed a muddy old potato riddler with another old farmer standing at the back of it. We stood our bikes up and asked if I could get some photos of them working; they kindly agreed. It was a cracking subject, the farmer was shovelling potatoes on to the conveyer belt, and the older man at the back was picking them out. Behind this was a complex of old barns. This sparked my imagination instantly and when we got home I prepared a big 40x30" linen canvas to paint on. The next morning, Dad and I cycled back to the barns. I was sitting at the entrance to the farm painting a small oil sketch when the older farmer, Will, dressed in an old patched up, grey mac, tied around the middle with a piece of baling twine, approached us. After watching me painting and having a chat, Will told me I could paint anywhere on his farm. I have been a permanent feature since that day!

I do countless oil sketches of their farm throughout the seasons. It is an artist's delight! Ancient red-brick barns stacked high with bales. Old tractors resting in front. Lovely dark barn interiors and a couple of straw stacks outside covered by a tarpaulin where stands the old orange potato riddler. I have done several large paintings of Will and John Puncher riddling the potatoes. And another nice one of Will Puncher taking potatoes out of a sack. There are unlimited painting opportunities at the farm and the Puncher brothers are so kind to allow me to paint and photograph them and their farm. I cannot thank them enough.

I feel that with these paintings of the brothers I'm capturing a way of life that, unfortunately, will disappear in my lifetime. It's a happy-sad feeling: I have captured the brothers and their way of life on their farm and hopefully my paintings will be around for hundreds of years to come. But it's sad that they are the last of their breed and these characters and their gentle way of farming will never be brought back.

My paintings of them are not a photographic reproduction. They are impressions, a record of the feelings, of the light and movement. The brothers afford me a valuable moment in their seasonal jobs within the farm such as potato riddling and ploughing.

It is important to me too that I do not pose them. None of my subjects are posed. I don't tell them to stand exactly like this and move their arm up, yes just a little higher and place your right leg a little lower. It's not like that, it's key to have them as they are in all the charm of their own posture and the way that they walk or stand is unique to each individual. This is vital in capturing their character.

I have said that I have painted a way of life that will disappear, and I think it's the same for my landscapes. Nothing stays the same forever and I've witnessed barns and meadows that I've painted being renovated and turned into homes and gardens, and new houses have replaced the locations that I used to paint and enjoy. Lovely wooden boats, an art form in themselves, have been overthrown by ugly, plastic boats that don't have the same charm. That's happened within my relatively short life. I worry sometimes what I'll be painting in years to come if things continue the way they are.

BILLIE AND BEAU IN THE SNOW
24x18", oil on canvas

Beau (pronounced 'Bo') makes her first appearance in this painting. The light was just beautiful, it had a yellow tinge to it which worked well and contrasted with the cerulean blue shadows. I worked from a photo as I'm almost certain Bille wouldn't stand, freezing, for two hours – nor would the snow last that long!

THE BRIDGE PONT
12x12", oil on board

My landscapes are all painted either plein air or from sketches or photographs that I've taken. I couldn't imagine myself preparing a palette or canvas ready to paint something I have imagined or completely made up! However I do exercise a little artistic license, for example, I choose to omit electricity pylons and wind turbines.

I'm fortunate in the fact that I don't have a problem in letting my paintings go. Usually they stand around in my studio for great lengths of time before an exhibition and I see them everyday. So when they're sold and delivered to their new homes I don't feel sad but excited that this leaves me to paint new scenes. I do keep a few paintings for myself, typically paintings that hold good memories, or pictures of friends and family.

BOWL OF APPLES AND A BLUEBELL
7x10", oil on board

Every now and then I like to do a still life, although it is almost the opposite to what attracts me to paint, which is light and movement. There is no movement in still life and the light is often artificial. I also find arranging a still life composition awkward. But this painting worked well!

The paintings that stick in my memory are ones that show a big leap of improvement or ones that I'm totally happy with, which is rare! Paintings like, 'Mending the Pots, Newlyn' depicting our good friend Bill, a Mousehole fisherman, is a favourite. I think it was this painting that marked the start of my new era of figurative work. It was a month's work, working on it at least four hours a day. The time and effort paid off. Works like 'Sons of the Soil' and 'One Too Many' reflect how important to me it is capturing the impression of the subjects' stance and the way they work within the landscape.

I also try to sketch and paint still life compositions. Especially during winter months or in moments when I've reached saturation point on other subjects. Fruit, bottles and flowers are commonplace in my work, things that can be found readily in the house. This is simply an exercise to hone my drawing skills with paint. I also enjoy making a subject up that hasn't sprung from the landscape. This helps to open my eyes again to the landscapes around me after taking a short break from painting them.

I also try to paint scenes that do not include a sky or horizon. Creating studies of geese, sheep, cattle, figures, horses, streams, boats etc. I was told at a young age that everyone can paint, but not everyone can draw and the best artists give the best advice and that is to draw,

BUTLER TAKING FIVE
14x10", oil on board

I got the photo of this man whilst in the kitchen on a tour of the house at Blickling at Christmas. He was reading an old paper with the headline "Our new King will be forty one on Monday". I like the understated surroundings and the flecks of light catching the form of the chair.

MONOCHROME STUDY OF FARMER
8.75x8", watercolour with body-colour

29

FIRST SNOW THORNAGE
5"x9", pastel

to draw until you are sick of drawing, then draw some more. I enjoy pencil sketching especially in the evenings.

I work with watercolours and pastels, as well as oil. I don't particularly have a favourite medium. All the three mediums offer something different and unique. I work on Arches 400lb rough watercolour paper stretched down on to a board to avoid cockling, but I've now started to use again Langton watercolour pads about 10x14" size. 200lb is perfect for location sketches. The watercolour pads allow the paints to dry really quickly but they don't allow too many washes.

The medium of watercolour is beautiful. It's very unforgiving and you cannot make a mistake. It's about achieving the painting in one hit and watercolour doesn't lend itself to faffing about. That's why I like it. The medium also has a great history and I love seeing it used well, in the works of Walter Langley especially. He excelled in mastering the subtlety of portraiture in the trickiest medium, especially in his large paintings of his model 'old Grace'. I spend a lot of time in Penlee House Gallery, Penzance studying his watercolours. They often have a deep emotional response to the life of fishing families. He painted the hardship and tragedy of life, like his painting 'Among the Missing – Scene in a Cornish Fishing Village'.

My favourite Walter Langley painting is 'Waiting for the Boats'. It is a masterpiece, showcasing his exquisite technical ability to portray the human form.

WALTER LANGLEY (1852-1922)
'IN THE EVENING OF LIFE'
14x10", watercolour

I find pastels equally different and enjoyable. They're very messy and can get muddy easily. I like using them because the colours are vivid; it's something I can't achieve with the other mediums. I work on fine sand paper, taped to a board. I use a range of soft chalk pastel brands from Senilliere to Schminke. I like George Clausen's pastel work, such as 'In the Rick Yard' and 'Head of a Young Girl (Rose Grimsdale)'. I like the way Clausen handled the pastel in a textural way, quite impressionistic. His pictures excel in rendering the appearance of things under flecking outdoor sunlight, or in the shady shelter of a barn or stable. I feel in his work he makes the very best of the composition. In his most well known works such as 'Winter Work' and 'Building the Rick' he best demonstrates this. I spend many hours looking at his work, seeing how he layered the oil paint up in his more impressionistic paintings such as 'Gleaners Coming Home', studying the faces of the farm labourers, the play of the reflected light on their faces from the wheat field, admiring the quality of his use of the square brush technique in 'The Ploughboy'. I feel you can learn a great deal by studying other people's paintings.

I attended primary school up to the end of Year 6. Although I enjoyed a lot about school – mainly break times and playing football – I just wanted to paint and school got in the way! For the past four years I've been educated at home, which has been one of the best decisions we've made. It's given me the opportunity for painting to take priority, with school work and studying to fit in around the prime time for painting.

I'm able to choose subjects I enjoy. I love poetry and I find writing poetry and painting equally satisfying, as I'm often thinking of stanzas whilst I'm painting.

I feel you can learn a great deal by studying other people's paintings.

Jonathan Smith quoted A. J. Munnings in *Summer in February* as saying 'poems are paintings I keep in my mind'. Munnings also admitted that if he had to choose between keeping paintings in his house or books, that he would most certainly have chosen books.

Having a house full of paintings is as important to me as being outdoors seeing nature first hand. Paintings are like windows, and I could never be without them. I enjoy collecting artwork, and with Dad buying and selling artwork, there is always a multitude of auction catalogues arriving through the letterbox. As a family we all have a visual appreciation and we thrive on soaking up landscapes – that's why we love Cornwall so much. And although my parents don't paint, they appreciate art and equally enjoy seeing the same things I do when we're out and about. Often for example they'll see a seascape and they'll know what medium I would best use to capture it. I couldn't achieve what I do without that understanding. They may not fully understand what goes on in my mind, but they know and respect how important it is to me. I'm fortunate at my age to have had my efforts validated. I thank my sister especially for her cooperation and forgiveness each time we pull over in the car to take photos!

So I'll continue on my journey appreciating the never-ending flow of inspiration. From those first few days spent on Cornish soil, seeing the light that sparkled upon a turquoise sea, that made me the artist I am, I must stay true to that. And I'll continue to appreciate the lure of The Broads reflecting those beautiful imposing skies that equally capture my heart. And may there be many more skies, seas and streets in-between these two counties that will continue to unveil their stories to me.

I love poetry and I find writing poetry and painting equally satisfying.

Family photo.

WET SOCKS
18x24", oil on canvas

I spotted this stunning subject whilst walking to Marazion. I'd seen the horses whilst still on the outskirts of Penzance. I ran along the beach, jumping over the rivulets of water, making my career as an Olympian, trying to catch up with the horses! As I got to them the light started to shine, I was really pleased to see a grey dappled horse – the best looking horses – whenever I see one I have to paint it!

WALK ALONG TRELISSICK ESTATE
16x22", oil on canvas

I took the photo of these horse from the window of a holiday cottage. I was dying to paint them but the background behind was an ugly building. So I put the horses into a Cornish landscape, about 2 miles from where the holiday cottage was. The two subjects worked very well. I loved painting the green reflected light and muscle tones in the horses.

WINTER START MUNDESLEY
10.5x15.5", watercolour

This scene is often viewed whilst walking along the beach at Mundesley in Norfolk. It always gives me inspiration to paint.

SUMMER AT FOWEY
7x10", watercolour

The Ploughman's Knot.

Sketches of Mr Flood
knot 7

THE PLOUGHMAN'S KNOT
18x24", oil on canvas

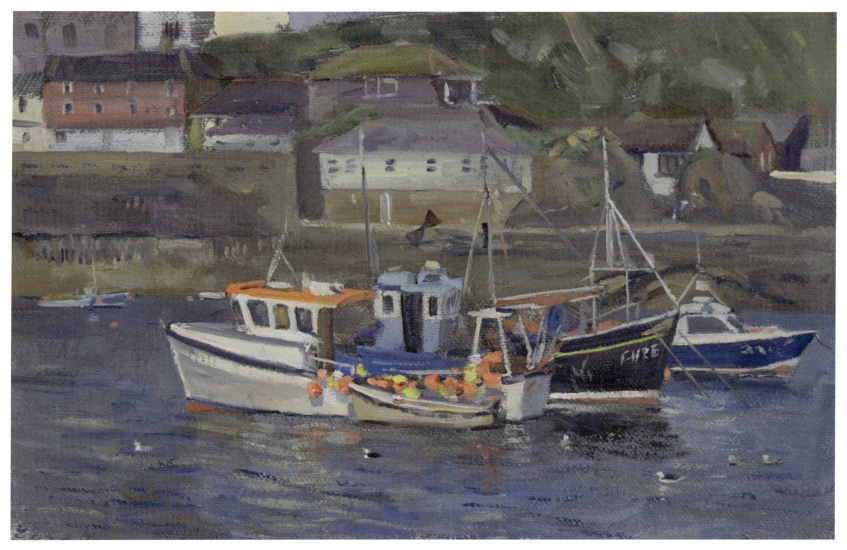

MOORED VESSELS MEVAGISSEY
6x9", oil on board

I painted this on a breezy morning after arriving by ferry in Mevagissey, from Fowey. The breeze carried a freezing chill. I enjoyed painting this, though I needed more clothing than a shirt and shorts!

Opposite:
HARBOUR MOUTH SWELL
8x8", oil on board

The boat coming into the harbour was struggling against the swell that was thrusting it out of the harbour. The colour of the water was a steely blue with almost pure viridian green reflections, which gave an unusual tonal combination.

PASSING RAIN CLOUDS
6x9", oil on board

What a beautiful sky this was! The cloud keeps your eye in the painting and counterbalances the blue shadows upon the stubble.

A CORNISH HEDGEROW
6x8", oil on board

I tucked in behind a wall to escape the wind and approaching rain. For a short time the sun shone and lit up the wall nicely.

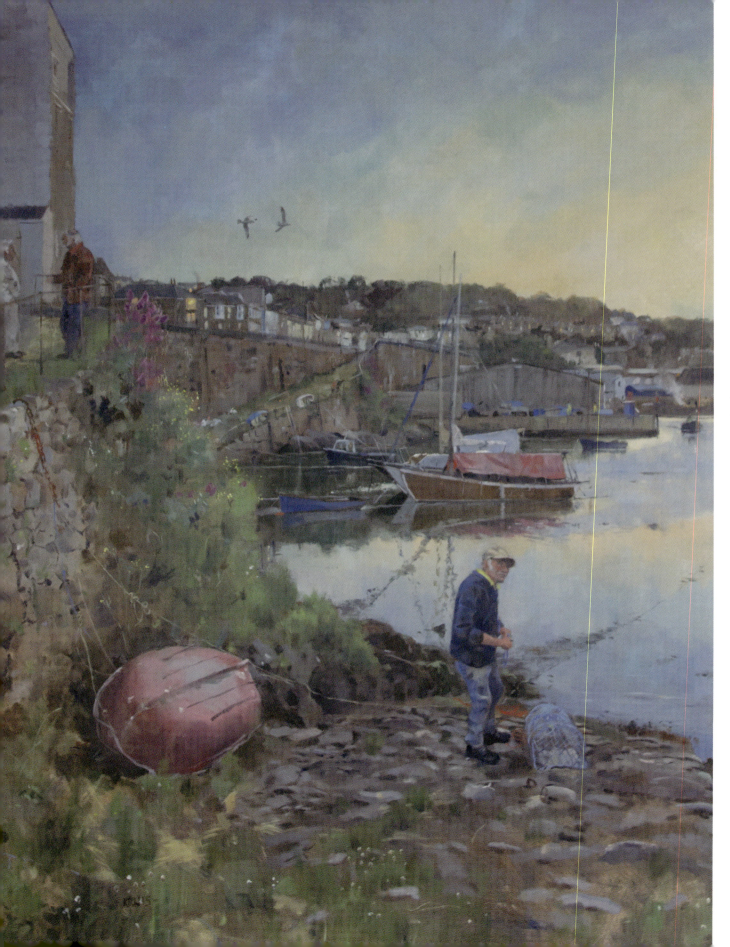

MENDING THE POTS, NEWLYN
40x30", oil on canvas

This painting was the beginning of my progression into large figurative work. Painted in the weeks after returning from Cornwall in 2014, after seeing 'Cornish Light, the Nottingham 1894 Exhibition Revisited', at Penlee House. I was full of Stanhope Forbes and the Newlyn School. The scene here depicts Newlyn old harbour as the sun drops behind the hillside. The fisherman is our friend Bill, from Mousehole. The painting took me a month to paint, spending about six hours a day working on it.

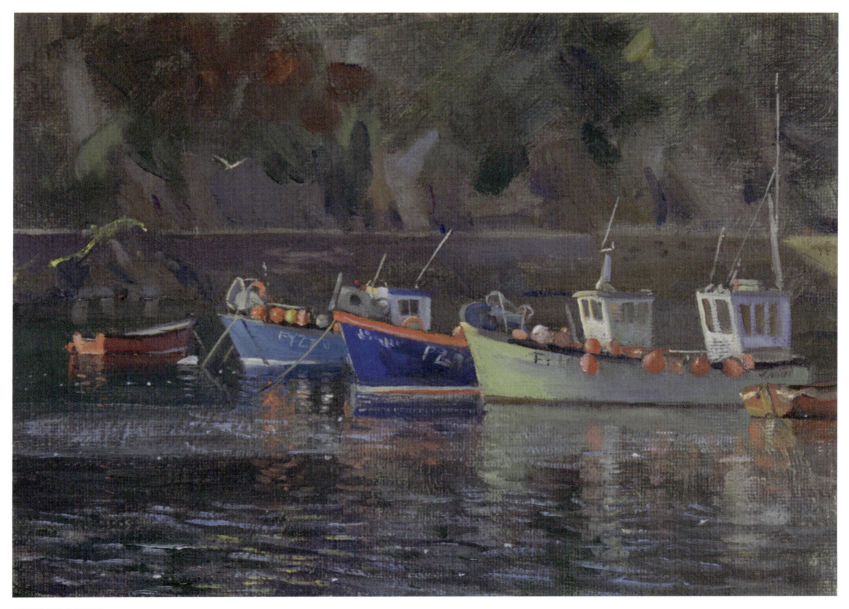

SUNLIT BOWS
size 6x8", oil board

This was a joy to paint. Everything went well. It was such a beautiful subject; I like the rich colours.

VIEWS OF THE WORLD
24x20", oil on canvas

These jovial characters were more than happy to have their photograph taken, which was a relief! I painted this complex painting on our return from Cornwall in October. I did get lost in the moment and put in every detail!

THE DRESSERS
30x20", oil on board

MID HARVEST
8x10.5", watercolour

I enjoyed a period of two weeks painting almost entirely plein air. The resulting watercolours have improved my work greatly. I love the colours in this. Viewed from Trunch over the fields to Southrepps.

Opposite:
BALES BEFORE BRADFIELD
8x10.5", watercolour

The Potato Shed

- KDW16 -

ONE TOO MANY
24x18", oil on canvas

This painting has set the standard of my work that follows. With the detail and level of work it's easy to make it disjointed. I like the light just glowing on the back wall.

SIXTY BLEATING SHEEP
18x24", oil on canvas

I'd much rather paint a horse or a cow over a sheep. But I couldn't resist painting this. After painting a dozen detailed sheep I realised what I'd let myself in for. I painted every sheep's face and every sheep's backside! The title for this painting came easily!

GRAZING SPRING PASTURES
12x16", oil on board

This beautiful subject was photographed a few years ago whilst I was painting bluebells in Blickling Wood (though I added the interesting sky from another photo).

SANDPOOLS , ST MICHAEL'S MOUNT
5x10", pastel

VIEW FROM A WINDOW
10x20", pastel

Opposite:
IRIDESCENT MORNING,
MEVAGISSEY
16x22", oil on canvas

The location sketch was the inspiration for this painting. I changed it slightly, adding the foreshore. The aim was to capture the amazing silver colours in my location sketch.

Right:
THE GOLDEN EVENING
SURRENDERS TO THE
SILVER NIGHT
14x11", oil on canvas

I got the photo for this after Dad woke me up about 10pm. Then Dad, my older sister and I walked into Fowey to get some photos. On our way back towards Readymoney Cove this brilliant scene presented itself. I loved painting the Polruan blockhouse illuminated by the light.

Frosty Scent

Opposite:
FROSTY SCENT
11x14", oil on canvas

I got the photograph for this at the Royal Norfolk Show. I changed the background to make it a better composition. I enjoyed painting the hounds scampering along.

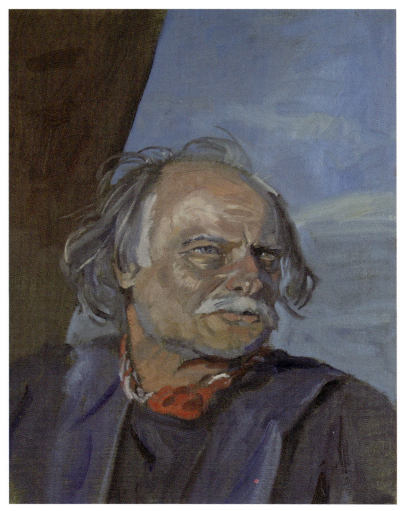

A SAILOR'S FACE
12x9", oil on board

This portrait of Tim captures the moment we were being towed back into Mousehole harbour by fishermen, a look of relief cast upon his weathered face.

Opposite:
SNAGGED MAINSAIL
10x10", oil on board

I made this portrait of Tim Pender while in a holiday cottage, housebound due to relentless rain and wind. This depicts the moment Tim realises the mainsail had got snagged and after his hat blew into the sea!

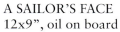

SUNBURST OVER HAPPISBURGH
11x14", oil on canvas

I see this view regularly as we walk our dog at Mundesley. The attraction to paint this was the atmosphere. Happisburgh church looms out of the mist as the clouds momentarily break.

SEA SPRAY
6x8", oil on board

I painted this just out of reach of the waves, but in the firing line of the relentless wind. I like how the wet shining cliff echoes the form of the sea.

SILVER SUN FOWEY
7x5", oil on board

After walking back to Readymoney Cove from the harbour at Fowey, the sun began to glow through the fog. Dad and I rushed up to St Catherine's castle and I painted this sitting on a bench just above it. I am fond of this painting as I was eating a beautiful saffron bun, bought from a bakery in the harbour.

I love the light in Cornwall. It is very silvery and intense. The landscapes are the complete opposite to Norfolk.

DUSKY ORANGES
6x9", oil on board

The night before I painted this I jokingly said to Dad 'Do you want to go out painting in Mevagissey tomorrow morning? The weather looks as if it's going to be good.' And I thought nothing else of it, until I got woken up early the following morning by Dad who asked 'Do you want to go out painting in Mevagissey? The weather looks good.'

So as we (Dad, my older sister and I), walked down into the harbour, after driving from Fowey, the smell of bakeries cooking and the sounds of seagulls filled the air. It was the most incredible light I've ever seen. Painted about half an hour before sunrise. The sea took on a silvery blue-yellow. The subject was so amazing it was already half-painted in my mind. This was the sketch for a larger painting, completed in Norfolk.

FARM GEESE STUDY
24"x18", oil on board

CHAROLAIS BULL
11x14", oil on canvas

The challenge here was not making the bull too colourful! A lot of colours were reflected on it's body: reds, ochres, blues and greens. Though I enjoyed the challenge, the colours help define the muscle shapes.

ESTUARY VIEW
4.75x7", watercolour

STILL MORNING
7x10.75", watercolour

Such a beautiful and still morning couldn't be missed. I did this very simple watercolour. This reminded me of several Seago paintings of Pin Mill and The Broads.

ROOKS RETREAT
7x10", oil on board

AUTUMN TREADS WHERE SUMMER RAN
7x10", oil on board

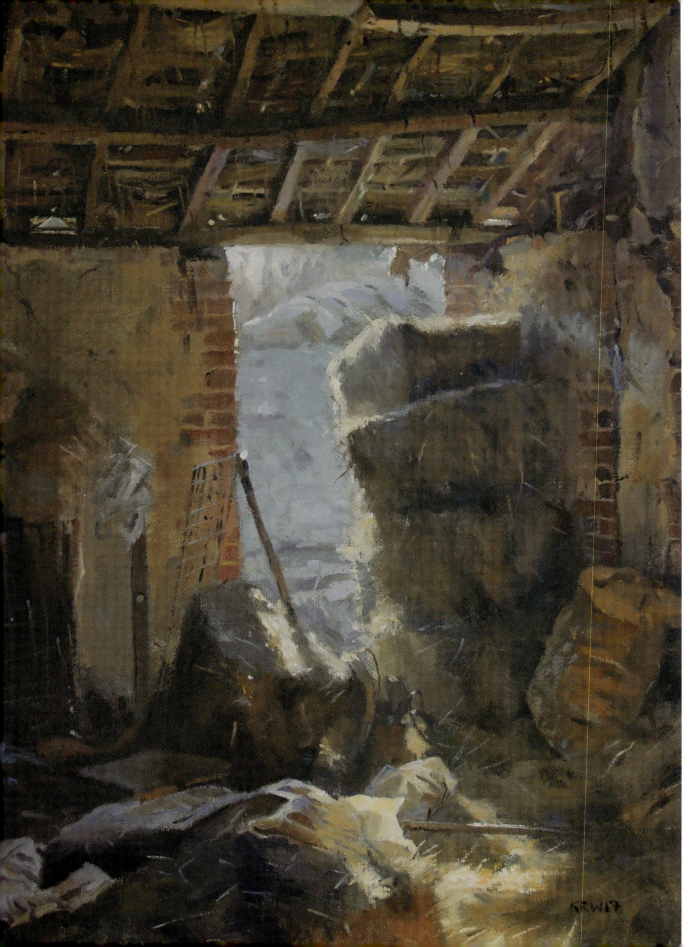

GOLDEN BARN
14x10", oil on board

This was just the most stunning barn interior. I have never enjoyed a painting experience more. It's not often you get to appreciate the interior of a barn untouched by developers.

Opposite:
IT WAS QUIET
7x10", oil on board

This was one of the coldest mornings Dad and I have been out painting in. I painted this two days before Christmas and the song 'Ring out Solstice Bells' was playing in my head.

SHELTERED MOORINGS MOUSEHOLE
8x10.5", watercolour

Opposite:
EVENING SUN, NEWLYN
8x11", watercolour

GOLDEN STUBBLE
7x10", oil on board

I painted this on a cloudless evening about 7:30 pm. The light was pure yellow and everything glowed.

Rustic Shades of Autumn

Bales lay scattered in golden fields, crowned by squawking crow.
Apricot tones of setting sun, acknowledge defeat and beyond the horizon glow.

Warm not the skeletal trees of charcoal grey, with dusk approaching they now embrace.
And herds of deer canter into the shadows, as the harvest moon ascends with grace.

And now with moon cast high above silent stage, Jack performs his merry play.
And casts his carpet of silver needles enveloping the bales that quietly lay.

Through the night he plots and plans, his endearing play well-known.
And although a million diamonds sparkle, beneath still hides the rust-clad tone.

White now is the slowly rising sun, lacklustre in its performance and weak.
No strength left to burn but enough to encourage the last amber tones to peek.

The field of russet globes comes alive with children dancing.
Harvesting their trophies they chant, the excitement in the chilly air enhancing.

As nine o'clock cometh, no pumpkin left uncarved, alone or unused.
The eery night intensifies with apprehension, clearly bemused.

And as the first lights appear of sparking wood, and firework a plenty.
Golden globes flicker with fear of spells, many more so than five and twenty.

Gradually appears one by one, glowing faces, as an approaching swarm.
Finally, fireside the children gather, with the chatter of teeth, huddled to keep warm.

Sipping at steaming pumpkin soup, and roasting chestnuts in pans of copper bright.
With orange and yellow flames licking at glasses, oh 'tis a warming sight!

For tonight is for joy, and not for grimacing nor for feeling sorrow.
But the farmer knows in his heart his day will be hard tomorrow.

And so it is with farmer out on the freezing marsh, the reluctant cattle do walk.
Towards barns of hay across the field where the pink foot geese stay and talk.

Bales lay scattered in golden fields, crowned by squawking crow.
Apricot tones of setting sun, acknowledge defeat and beyond the horizon glow.

BRISK WALK
20"x30", oil on board

Brown and white horses toss their manes,
Along the field, the snowy plane;
And the winter winds be moaning

DUCKS CROSSING
12"x16", oil on board

CHRISTMAS
NOSTALGIA
12x9", oil on canvas

*This stunning subject I
photographed at Blickling
one wintry evening before
Christmas. I love the halo
of light on the people in the
carriage. After I finished it
I was reminded of some
John Atkinson Grimshaw
paintings.*

AUTUMN'S GOLDEN SHADES
8x10", oil on canvas

I painted this on our first painting trip with our new dog Beau. She behaved well but didn't appear in this painting!

OCHRE FIELDS
6.75x10", watercolour and body colour

FARMSTEAD, LAMORNA
5.75x8.5", watercolour

I painted this on a wet afternoon in a holiday cottage. I worked from a photograph Mum and Dad took whilst on a walk. It is nice to see the old granite farmsteads still standing and in use.

MOUSEHOLE
7x10", oil on board

STORM APPROACHING ST MICHAEL'S MOUNT
5x7", oil on board

I painted this one evening after a day of sunshine and showers. The light fell perfectly but briefly upon the Mount. Julius Olsson was a looming inspiration in this. This painting is only 5x7 inches but could easily be ten times as big.

TANGERINE DAWN
7x5", oil on board

This needed paint straight out of the tube, because the sky was so bright.

LIGHT SHARD, COLD HARBOUR
4.75x6.5", pastel

The attraction to paint this was the eerie atmosphere, the sun just showing in the gloomy sky. It reminds me of a Clausen oil of a horse and cart in the mist (see page 144).

DECEMBER IN JUNE
8x12", oil on board

Painted whilst being filmed by the BBC alongside David Curtis. It was absolutely freezing and a shock after spending two nice weeks in Cornwall a couple of days before painting this. Completely unlike June weather, hence the title.

Opposite:
DISTANT CATTLE
10x14", oil on board

Painted entirely on site from a bench at How Hill sitting alongside painter friend, Tony Garner. The aim was to capture the light and shadows that fall over the marshes on a partly cloudy day.

BROADLAND MIST
6"x9", pastel

STILL LIGHT ST BENET'S
9x9", watercolour

GOLDEN HALO
8x12", oil on board

DECEMBER WALK
16x12", oil on board

I don't usually like the rugs on horses, I find it obscures the shape of the animal, but the light was too good not to paint.

Sketch for December walk

GATHERING CLOUDS
8x12", oil on board

The skies around harvest time are amazing, captured here in my painting.

Opposite:
SCUDDING CLOUDS
9x12", oil on board

I did a small watercolour sketch for this. I was pleased to see that the trees, painted with the palette knife, worked well.

GLOWING DAWN
8x12", oil on board

With Norfolk being my home county there is undoubtedly a bond with the landscape I have grown up with.

Opposite:
ERIC EDWARDS, REEDCUTTER
10X10", oil on board

AMONG THE FIELD OF SNOW
9.25x6.25", pastel

I painted this from a photo we took about ten years ago when we lived in Holt. The winters always seemed so snowy. My memories are that we spent all our time in the fields past Spout Hills, along the railway track to "the enchanted wood", continuing along the fields to Letheringsett.
This painting captures the nostalgia of memories brought to mind.

I work on no particular places first, only saving my favourite bits until last.

WATERSIDE SHARDS BURGH
5.5x5.5", pastel

EVENING CAST SHADOWS
5.75x8.75", watercolour

I photographed this from the car coming back to Port Isaac after a day out in Boscastle. The light was lovely and strong, typical of late autumn evenings.

Opposite:
VIEWS OVER POLRUAN – KINGS WALK
7.75x5.75", watercolour

One of my favourite haunts whenever we stay in Fowey. I love the whole design in this composition, enhanced by the colours: greys, greens and ochres.

JUNE RIDE
10x8", oil on canvas

What a fantastic subject. Spotted on our first day staying in a place on Restronguet Creek. I was in my element with horses, cattle, boats and estuaries all in a close proximity to the holiday cottage. The lady is glancing over the bridge towards the creek and is riding a stunning grey dappled horse. I got another photo of the lady on the horse but side on; I've persuaded myself to paint it.

Opposite:
DAPPLED GREY HORSE
16x20", oil board

Since writing about 'June ride' I've kept my word and painted this. My third attempt at this exact subject and I have finally got it right! I love the horse, the crimson reflected light on its underbelly and hind-quarters. The rider's clothes really complemented the colour palette of the painting – a red top wouldn't have worked.

BLUE BONNET
7x10", oil on board

I was losing in this painting, nothing was going well. I continued with it and when I got home it was turned to face the wall and left for a few days. Looking at it with fresh eyes, it didn't look too bad. I altered a few things and now I'm quite happy with it!

BLOSSOMING HEDGEROW
7x10", oil on board

I painted this whilst being filmed by Natalie Gray for an ITV piece. I love painting blossom and in this farmyard setting with the riddler, everything was perfect.

FROST FARMSTEAD
7x10", oil on board

I loved the clouds in the sky, making this frosty scene really moody. I can't tell you how freezing it was painting this!
I like the foreground mass of decaying plants touched by frost.

Opposite:
SUNLIT COPSE
7x10", oil on board

I found this subject the day before by chance. I knew the sun would rise around the copse. Dad and I arrived the next morning and I painted it. I was pleased with the result and would like to do a bigger one and add the sheep that were grazing behind the gate that I didn't include here.

WINTER SHEEP AT BURGH
4.5x7", pastel

I enjoyed painting this pastel. The limited palette of varying grey tones worked really well.

FIELD VIEWS TOWARDS LETHERINGSETT
5x8", pastel

Snow always works well in pastel: the crispness of pastel I think makes that succeed. This view is of the fields from Holt to Letheringsett.

HARVEST GLOW
6x9", watercolour and body-colour

THE SMOKING STOVE
6.75x7", watercolour and body-colour

SUNSHINE BEFORE A STORM
7x10", oil on board

We stayed in Port Isaac for three weeks in September and didn't get much more than wind and rain! I seized any opportunity when the sun did shine, to paint or swim. Although swimming was limited by the invasion of the Portuguese man-of-war jellyfish, brought in by the bad weather.

READYMONEY MORNING
7x10", oil on board

I seem to paint before sunrise quite often for some reason. A lot of my paintings occupy the half an hour before and after sunrise. I like the greys and oranges and pinks that glow and reflect in the landscape. In this painting I love the wet sand reflecting the sky.

SONS OF THE SOIL
30x20", oil on board

I love this painting, I think because the composition is so striking. The scene was spotted by chance whilst cycling through Knapton. The two brothers amble across the field to their tractor. The field is to be set with potatoes.

THE RIDDLERS
40x30", oil on canvas

I was inspired completely by the rustic charm of this grey weathered painting – my mind full of George Clausen's rustics in his countryside paintings, of Bastien-Lepage's paintings of peasants, and James Guthrie's 'A Hind's Daughter'. I put everything into creating a nostalgic rural scene, in the depths of Norfolk.

LATE FOR LUNCH
7x10", oil on board

This was the location sketch for "Farm Fresh Potatoes".

I work with watercolours and pastels, as well as oil. I don't particularly have a favourite one.

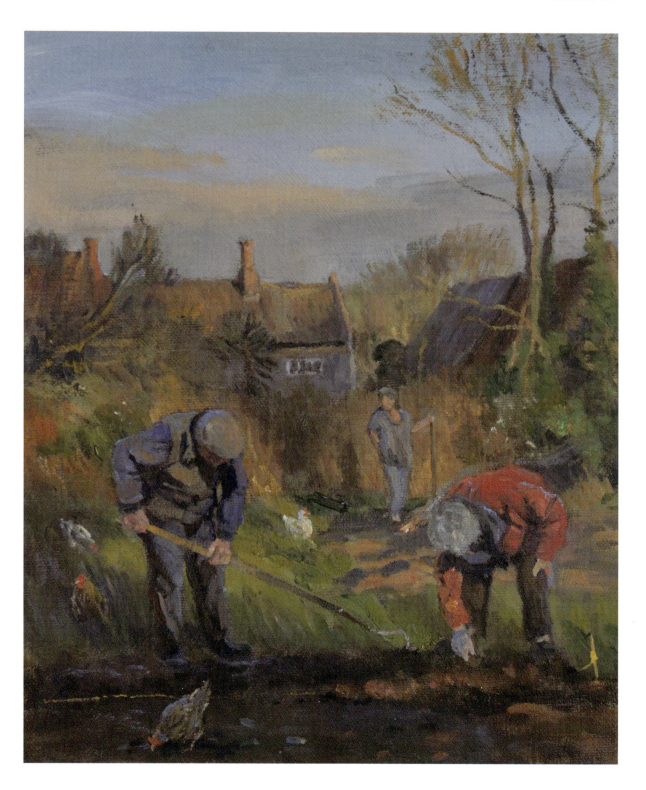

POTATO PATCH, SPRING
10x8", oil on board

Clausen was a huge inspiration when I painted this. Our next door neighbours let me photograph them setting potatoes. I changed the background to the allotment down the road.

FOXGLOVES UNDER EVENING SHADES
10x12", oil on canvas

I spotted this subject on the first day staying on a farm in St Juliot's near Boscastle. There is a lovely statuesque form to foxgloves. I'm not a botanical artist but I loved painting the cone-shaped flowers.

BILLIE & BLUEBELLS
6x8", oil on board

I got the inspiration for this after seeing a Henry Scott Tuke painting. The composition worked well and I thankfully avoided it being too twee.

FOAMING SEA ST CLEMENTS
6.5x9.5", watercolour and body-colour

TURQUOISE HAZE
6.75x9.75", watercolour

As the storm cleared I painted this from the holiday cottage window. The horizon was hazy and the sea and the sky had no line of change.

OCTOBER MIST
7x10", oil on board

While painting this I had a few lines of a poem going through my head. Once I got home I wrote a haiku poem about this painting:

The dank mist hangs low
Dew-laden leaves fall in to the stream
Where the fast currents run.

Opposite:
MY CHOSEN PATH
14x10", oil on board

THE WHITE PONY
9x12", oil on canvas

I really enjoy painting subjects like this, especially the muscle tones and reflected light, causing the horse's belly to take on a green tinge.
I used the palette knife to catch the light on the horse's back.

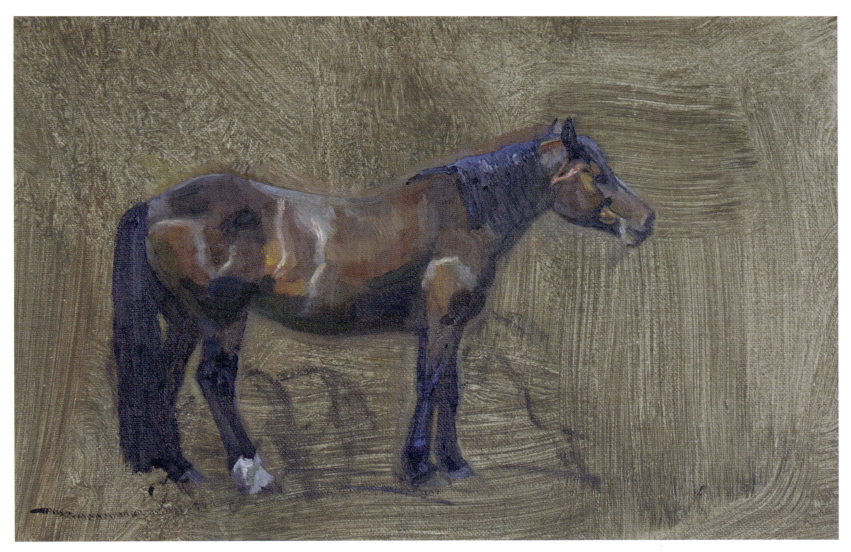

SHINING COAT
8x12", oil on board

This stunning horse had to be painted. The light shone beautifully on its body and only enhanced its looks.

MEANDERING RIVULETS
7x10", oil on board

Opposite:
WINDING TO THE SEA
7x10", oil on board

Right:
WILL PUNCHER, LATE SUMMER
16x12", oil on board

*This was inspired by a George Clausen
painting 'The Birds Nest'. I used the
impressionistic style of vivid colours
layered on top of each other to create the
complexion of Will's skin.*

Opposite:
MR FLOOD AND HIS HORSES
16x16", oil on board

MEVAGISSEY MORNING LIGHT
5x9.5", pastel

I like the contrast between the deep blue sea and the bright light sky.

GULLS AFORE ST MICHAEL'S MOUNT
5.5x8.75", pastel

HARVEST FIELDS
8x10", watercolour

This is my favourite in the series of harvest watercolours. I painted this on a Sunday afternoon after playing football. I painted to the sounds of cricketers at Bradfield, cattle mooing in the field behind the trees and a music festival happening at the Gunton Arms.

Opposite:
CHURCH AND CROWS
7x10", watercolour

SCULLING MEVAGISSEY
14x10", oil on board

Opposite:
CADMIUMS AND COBALTS
14x10", oil on board

I painted this from sketches I made on location. I like the simple composition and lovely colours.

I love to find hidden subjects, things that people haven't painted.

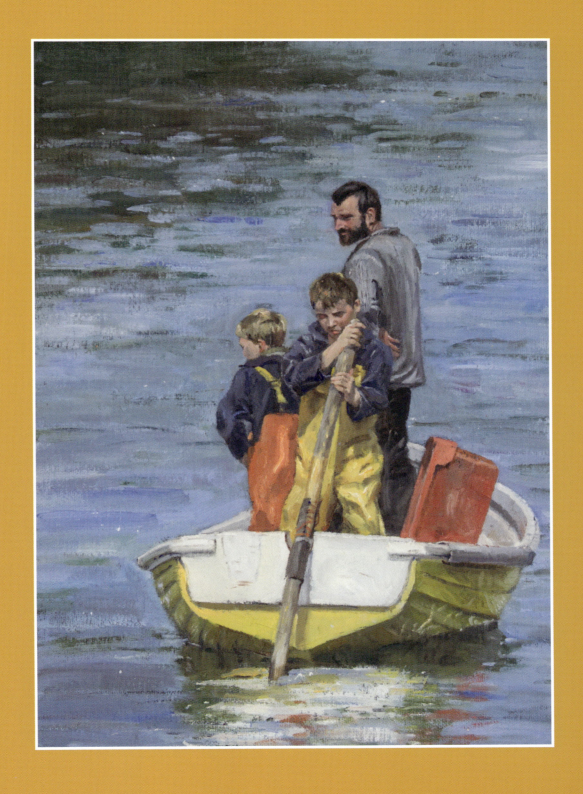

A GLIMPSE OF SUN
6x8", oil on board

Painted below the Old Coastguard Hotel, Mousehole, early on an August morning. The dolphins had chased the mackerel that had chased the pilchards towards the shore which were stranded as the tide receded. So for a few days the beach smelt unpleasantly of fermenting pilchards!

Kieron – An Outside View
by Simon Butler

SOMETIME AROUND 2009 I visited an exhibition with my late friend, the artist Michael Morgan RI. There was a flurry of interest around a particular painting, a landscape watercolour, surrounded by people examining it closely before standing back. Michael and I listened in on their conversations which mostly went along the following lines: 'And he's only seven and he's already selling for thousands...' – or 'There's all this fuss just because he's only seven...'. As we walked away I looked at Michael, waiting for response: 'What's age got to do with art,' is all he said.

Well, for Kieron Williamson, the popular media certainly led on the subject of age, most stories being of the 'Mini Monet' type, and more often than not referring to the sums being paid for his work. Only a few took time to consider the paintings themselves.

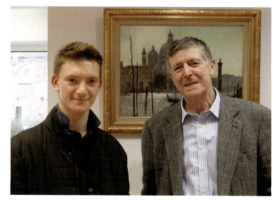

Kieron and Simon Butler at Adrian Hill Fine Art Gallery, Norfolk, in 2018.

For my part, having a career working with artists through collecting, publishing and staging exhibitions, I confess to keeping my fingers crossed as to Kieron's future success as a painter, not through misgiving about his talent, but in his ability to navigate at such a young age the pressures and perils of celebrity and considerable income – concerns that his gallery owner and I confided to each other when discussing exhibitions and the publication of Kieron's first book.

Such fears were unfounded. Now, at the grand old age of sixteen, Kieron shows no sign of letting success go to his head – in no small part due to the careful parenting of Keith and Michelle whose own concerns about bringing up a child at the centre of the world's focus, and the effect of that on the family, including Kieron's younger sister Billie-Jo, were made clear by Michelle in the book *Coming to Light*, which I published in 2012. 'As parents we do not look at Kieron's situation through commercial eyes... We don't know if we are making the right move, or the right decisions, to meet Kieron's wishes. So we have to trust our judgement and carry on as we are.'

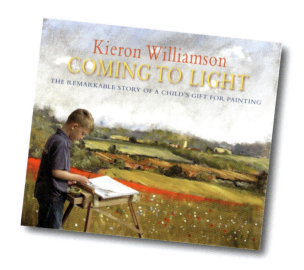

Assaulted from all sides with media attention, input from professional advisors, friends and family, and endless public scrutiny, the pressure became too much: 'Our life before had been simple and poor, but so rewarding. We wanted that back. The Kieron phenomenon had become too big for us... Media events and future sales and exhibitions were all cancelled in a frantic attempt to survive. We went into meltdown.'

Kieron when I first met him.

'Art is about communication and Kieron speaks to us unequivocally.'

Ken Howard OBE, RA

An early pastel and the first of Kieron's painting I saw.

For those outside the media arena it is difficult to imagine that such celebrity and success could be met with anything other than pleasure, but relentless scrutiny on a quiet family not given to showiness or self-approval, threatened the emotional fabric of their lives. The one least affected was Kieron himself, or so it seemed to an outsider – not that he wished to draw attention to himself either but simply because he was proud of his work and pleased that others like it too. For him, painting was already a passion. But what the world wanted to know was how long would the passion last?

It was just before the media storm broke that, while visiting Adrian Hill of Picturecraft Gallery in Holt, Norfolk, I saw my first Kieron painting, a pastel. Without telling me who it was by, Adrian asked my opinion. It was most unlike anything he usually exhibited in his gallery and I was intrigued, for while the picture had obvious childlike qualities it also exhibited elements that suggested to me a more mature hand, not least in the handling of perspective, the road narrowing to the horizon and the line of telegraph poles receding – something normally absent from a child's drawing, as was the treatment of the sky, fading from pale to darker blue. The palette had a boldness about it, the golden sun-topped hedgerow on the right and, oddly, my first thought was of the Australian artist Sydney Nolan – perhaps the colours, certainly the simple figures and their bold slanting shadows. When Adrian confessed it was the work of a six-year-old my instincts told me here was something quite remarkable.

I later discovered that, as a collector and dealer himself, Kieron's father had long admired the work of Jack Cox, whose vibrant use of colour would have been seen by Kieron who also grew to appreciate this local artist's work. These influences, of having art in the home, should not be underestimated, for while innate talent is one thing, the inspiration gained from having paintings as part and parcel of life growing up normalises the creative urge in the young.

For Kieron, these early influences sprang from the artists of the Norwich School whose works echoed the landscape he was familiar with – the trademark 'wide skies' and the depiction of the people and places of Norfolk as it used to be, a world now almost lost but still to be discovered in remote corners of the county such as those sought out by Kieron on his early morning bicycle rides into the county's rural heart. Visits to the Norwich Castle Museum and Art Gallery introduced Kieron to the works of the 'greats' of the Norwich School, among them John Crome (1768-1821), John Sell Cotman (18782-1842) and John Berney Crome (1794-1842), all of whom captured the essence of the landscape in their Norfolk works.

In conversation with Kieron one senses deep appreciation of the quality of these paintings but also a sense of loss for landscapes that hold so much by way of untrammelled loveliness – a regret that they have passed. Almost certainly this has led Kieron to seek out subjects

'Harvest Field' by Jack Cox (1914–2007). Cox was self-taught having spent most of his life as a fisherman and lifeboatman of Wells in Norfolk. Like Kieron he shared a love of the Norwich School painters.

We do what we see – and as an aspirational young painter Kieron was inevtiably influenced by the paintings he saw at home along with those in local galleries and museums. John Sell Cotman's watercolour painting of the Gatehouse at Wiggenhall is typical of the lyrical documentary style of landscape works from the period.

'Boats in St Ives Harbour' by Julius Olsson (1864–1942) who painted in both Newlyn and St Ives, finding interest in the workaday aspects of the fishing community. Such is Kieron's passion for Cornwall that the family have made plans to move there.

that, within a generation, will also disappear – not through sentimentality but a passionate desire to record rural life and landscapes fast disappearing.

It was among the galleries and museum of the county that Kieron also began to discover the works of that later generation of artists, including Alfred Munnings (1878–1959) and Arnesby Brown (1866–1955) who themselves paved the way for the 'moderns', among them Jeffrey Camp RA (b.1923), Ian Houston (b.1934) and Edward Seago (1910-1974), the last of whom has made the greatest impression on Kieron. Like these, Kieron has a fondness for painting in the landscape, his plein air work capturing a freshness and a subtlety of light that is so much the essence of both his native Norfolk and the Cornish landscapes he more recently discovered.

For many painters, particularly when the scene is of a busy harbourside or perhaps at a bustling County Show, the presence of interested onlookers asking questions and making comments becomes something of a distraction. Not so for Kieron who has always taken pleasure in sharing his delight in painting with others. In May 2016 I had the pleasure of inviting Kieron and his family to Devon to take part in an exhibition held at Delamore Estate which annually raises funds for charity. Always prepared to cheerfully support worthy causes Kieron had previously, in 2011, provided a watercolour of Delamore House which was used on the exhibition's catalogue cover and raised considerable funds for St Luke's Hospice in Plymouth.

Kieron's love of painting en plein air.

The West Lodge, Delamore, South Devon. Painted in oil en plein air in May 2016 on a visit to the annual Delamore Arts exhibition.

On this second occasion Kieron elected to paint in the grounds of the house over a couple of days during the month-long exhibition which attracts around 10,000 visitors. I watched with some concern as Kieron set up his easel and began painting, soon to be surrounded by small groups and individuals looking over his shoulder and engaging him in conversation. While chatting away, the oil painting gradually took shape and in less than a day was completed. What was also most interesting to observe was his choice of subject – not the grand house with its impressive lake, but a small lodge house, complete with a washing line

Kieron painting the West Lodge at Delamore 2016.

in the garden – the artist's eye selecting to paint what most interested him rather than what the public might expect.

Indeed, such is Kieron's celebrity, especially in his home country, that he's seldom without attention wherever he happens to be working. At his exhibitions too, he's more often than not to be seen chatting with visitors about his paintings, disarmingly friendly and forever thanking those who offer praise for his work.

Likewise Kieron is quick to acknowledge the help and support provided by experienced artists, many of whom Kieron joined on trips into the Norfolk countryside or sat with in the studio where he was able to listen to advice and watch the techniques they applied to a variety of mediums: pastel, watercolour and oil. On occasions these sessions would take place in the Picturecraft Gallery or as part of a formal teaching sessions given by artists such as Bryan Ryder ROI and Tony Garner. Yet, while absorbing the lessons so generously given, Kieron was always eager to follow his own instincts as to subject and style.

It was these instincts that led Kieron away from concentrating on pure landscapes into tackling what even many mature artists never conquer, intimate portraits of people and animals. These figurative works are not formal portraits with 'sitters' but rather depict people and animals in what might best be described as 'their natural habitats' - farmers and

Kieron's success has enabled him to build an impressive collection of artworks, particularly the late nineteenth and early twentieth century works of Norfolk and Cornwall. From his early visits to Cornwall, in particular time spent at Penlee House Gallery, Kieron discovered an immediate empathy with the artists of the Newlyn School, among them Fred Hall (1860–1948) whose work 'One Winter's Morn' he now treasures. Right: Detail from Kieron's oil, 'Brisk Walk'.

A pencil sketch by Lucy Kemp-Welch (1869–1958), now in Kieron's collection. Some of Kieron's own pencil work has been included in this book, drawings taken from his sketchbooks taken with him into the field.

fishermen, workhorses and cattle. Again, these are not sentimental pictures, although they often capture a world that is fast fading, as depicted in his portraits of the farming brothers at Knapton shown earlier in this book; it's more that they carry an unspoken narrative that strikes an immediate chord with the viewer.

Kieron's carefully chosen collection of fine art, made possible by the commercial success of his own paintings, is interesting to those looking for what might be a future direction for this young artist. His empathy with the works of the Newlyn School artists, for instance, is partly due to their allegorical content – for the stories they tell. But they also provide lessons in themselves for a young artist who can read in them the way in which each was constructed, the signature brush strokes, the creation of light and shade, the use of colour. These, Stanhope Forbes, Langley, Harris and Bramley among them, were masters of brush and canvas, and each reliant on the fundamental skill of draughtsmanship.

Technique is one thing but painting doesn't work unless the artist strives to reveal a truthfulness in their work, easily undone if the expertise is flawed. Painting people and animals is particularly demanding for it will be immediately obvious to the viewer if the figure is ill-conceived, be it man, woman or beast. First there's the anatomical accuracy, the general conformity of a figure bending to work, the musculature of a horse pulling a plough, the difference between the easy stance

'The Young Friends' by Stanhope Forbes (1857–1947). Forbes was an influential member of the Newlyn School and his Cornish paintings contain many of the elements that Kieron employs in his own work both stylistically and through narrative content. Note the easy stance of the young boy, captured perfectly.

Inset: detail from 'Shoeing the Horses' p.17.

143

Village Inn, Misty Morning' by George Clausen (1852–1944). Clausen is another important artist from whose work Kieron seeks both guidance and confirmation in the direction his own painting is taking. Already one finds in a number of works a move towards a more impressionistic approach.

Detail from Kieron's 'First Snow, Thornage'.

of a youth and the weary stoop in the shoulders of the work-worn farmer. And then there are the characteristics that define the individual – the ability of the artist to draw or paint a figure that makes them recognisable by name. Not always about the face, it's sometimes simply the tilt of the chin, the way the hands are held – so difficult to capture.

I called on the Williamson family early one February morning. Puddles lay frozen by the roadside and the endless flat Norfolk landscape was glazed with white. While I sat drinking coffee I was told that Kieron had set off on his bicycle at first light in order to paint the sunrise over the frosty fields. It's called dedication.

There is a cautionary tale in attempting to write about Kieron Williamson for so rapid is the development in one so young that whatever one writes today, may well change by tomorrow. Yet here, in the pictures in this book, we see all of these skills: mastering of technique, passion and dedication coming together. Here we can witness the development of an artist who is yet to reach full maturity and yet is showing the dedication and passion from which wonderful paintings are achieved. There's more to come and I for one will continue to wonder – what next?